Abraham Lincoln Abraham Linco
incoln Abraham Lincoln Abra
raham Lincoln Abraham Linco
incoln Abraham Lincoln Abra
raham Lincoln Abraham Linco
incoln Abraham Lincoln Abra
raham Lincoln Abraham Linco
incoln Abraham Lincoln Abra
raham Lincoln Abraham Linco
incoln Abraham Lincoln Abra
raham Lincoln Abraham Linco
incoln Abraham Lincoln Abra
raham Lincoln Abraham Linco

raham Lincoln Abraham Linco
incoln Abraham Lincoln Abra
braham Lincoln Abraham Linco
incoln Abraham Lincoln Abra
braham Lincoln Abraham Linco
incoln Abraham Lincoln Abra
braham Lincoln Abraham Linco
incoln Abraham Lincoln Abra
braham Lincoln Abraham Linco
incoln Abraham Lincoln Abra
braham Lincoln Abraham Linco
incoln Abraham Lincoln Abra
braham Lincoln Abraham Linco
incoln Abraham Lincoln Abra
braham Lincoln Abraham Linco
incoln Abraham Lincoln Abra
braham Lincoln Abraham Linco

A SHORT BIOGRAPHY OF ABRAHAM LINCOLN

A SHORT BIOGRAPHY OF
Abraham Lincoln

Erin Carlson Mast

🖋 **BENNA** BOOKS

Carlisle, Massachusetts

A Short Biography of Abraham Lincoln

Series Editor: Susan DeLand
Written by: Erin Carlson Mast

For Flynn and Schuyler

978-1-944038-25-0

Front cover: *Abraham Lincoln,* 1869
George P. A. Healy (1813–1894)
Oil on canvas, 73 ¾ in 55 ⅝ inches (187.3 x 141.3 cm)
Bequest of Mrs. Robert Todd Lincoln, 1939
White House Collection / White House Historical Association
939.1388.1
Back cover: *The Peacemakers,* 1868
George P. A. Healy (1813–1894)
Oil on canvas, 47 ⅛ x 62 inches (119.7 x 159.1 cm)
United States Government purchase, 1947
White House Collection / White House Historical Association
947.558.1
Left to right: Maj. Gen. William T. Sherman, Lt. Gen. Ulysses S. Grant,
President Abraham Lincoln, Rear Adm. David D. Porter

Published by Benna Books
an imprint of Applewood Books, Inc.
Carlisle, Massachusetts

To request a free copy of our current catalog
featuring our best-selling books, write to:
Applewood Books
P.O. Box 27
Carlisle, Massachusetts 01741
Or visit us on the web at: www.awb.com

10 9 8 7 6 5 4 3 2 1
MANUFACTURED IN THE UNITED STATES OF AMERICA

ABRAHAM LINCOLN, SIXTEENTH PRESIDENT of the United States, was born on February 12, 1809, in a one-room cabin at Sinking Spring Farm near Hodgenville, Kentucky. His journey from cabin to Executive Mansion was made possible by the unique system of democracy that exists in the United States. Abraham was the second child of Thomas Lincoln and Nancy Hanks Lincoln. Recounting his ancestry in a brief autobiography, he noted his parents were born in Virginia of "undistinguished families." His first known ancestor to cross the Atlantic from England was Samuel Lincoln, who moved from Hingham, Norfolk, to Hingham, Massachusetts, in 1638. Abe was named for his paternal grandfather, Captain Abraham Lincoln, who fought in the American Revolution. Captain Lincoln had survived the war and moved to Kentucky, only to be ambushed by Indians while he labored on his farm in 1786 and killed in front of his children. Thomas Lincoln was eight years old.

The origins of Abraham Lincoln's mother, Nancy Hanks Lincoln, are less certain. The prevailing belief is that she was the daughter of Lucy Hanks and Joseph Hanks, but no record of her birth has ever been found, fueling speculation that she was born out of wedlock.

Thomas and Nancy married in 1806 in Kentucky and welcomed their first child, Sarah, on February 10, 1807. Abraham came next, almost exactly two years after his sister. The decade that followed brought great misfortune: their third child, a son named Thomas, died in infancy. Then, on two separate occasions, Thomas

Lincoln's right to land—his livelihood—was challenged. In the first challenge, he lost all his land and had to uproot the family and start anew. In the second challenge, he retained a mere one-quarter of his claim.

In 1816, the Lincolns moved to Indiana, the year the territory became a state—a free state. Indiana offered more secure land rights. The Lincolns viewed slavery as economically unfair and, according to their Primitive Baptist faith, morally wrong. Abraham was accused later in life of being hostile toward Christianity, having particular disdain for the drama of religious revivals he witnessed in his youth. Yet his upbringing shaped his views on morality and predetermination. As president, Abraham noted that he was always against slavery.

> "I am naturally anti-slavery. If slavery is not wrong, nothing is wrong. I cannot remember when I did not so think, and feel."

Abraham's upbringing stands in stark contrast to that of most U.S. presidents who preceded him. George Washington was receiving a robust education and inherited slaves to do work for him by age eleven. Abraham was handed an ax at age eight to help clear the land for farming. Rather than sending his son to school, Thomas hired him out to others, taking his earnings, a common practice at the time. Abraham was schooled in skills necessary for frontier survival, though not necessarily with pleasure. Abraham claimed that after killing a wild turkey once, he never again pulled the trigger on larger game.

As president, Lincoln pardoned a Thanksgiving turkey, now a presidential tradition, after his youngest son begged him to spare the bird's life.

When Abraham was only nine, his mother Nancy fell ill and died of milk sickness, which occurs when someone ingests the flesh or dairy from a cow that ate the poisonous white snakeroot plant. Young Abraham helped build his mother's coffin, whittling the wooden pins that held the boards together. The family buried her in a clearing now known as Pioneer Cemetery.

A little over a year after Nancy's death, Thomas married Sarah "Sally" Bush Johnston, of Elizabethtown, Kentucky. Sally brought her three children, John, Elizabeth, and Matilda, from her first marriage with her. She insisted on significant improvements to the Lincoln family cabin, such as adding a wooden floor, a sleeping loft, and a roof that didn't leak on them as they slept. Sally treated the Lincoln children as her own, earning their affection.

Abraham's strength, height, and athleticism meant he was capable of hard labor; he simply had no interest in it. He earned a reputation for strength and bravery following a wrestling match with the leader of the notorious "Clary's Grove Boys," but he also earned a reputation for being lazy. Neighbors and family noted his lack of interest in manual labor and claimed that he spent all his time reading and writing. Sally did not deny her stepson showed far greater interest in learning—she nurtured it.

Abraham Lincoln received less than a

Sally Lincoln described Abraham as dutiful and kind, especially to animals and children.

year of formal education. In his 1859 brief autobiographical sketch, he employed his legendary wit to describe his early schooling:

> *"There were some schools, so called; but no qualification was ever required of a teacher beyond 'readin, writin, and cipherin' to the Rule of Three. If a straggler supposed to understand latin happened to sojourn in the neighborhood, he was looked upon as a wizzard* [sic]. *There was absolutely nothing to excite ambition for education."*

Sally filled the void, bringing with her a trove of books. Abraham eagerly read them all, including the King James Bible, *Aesop's Fables,* and *Lessons in Elocution.* His voracious appetite for books demonstrated his love of learning and his ambition to improve his lot in life.

As an adult, Lincoln enjoyed reading Shakespeare, declaring that nothing equals *Macbeth.*

Abraham's nineteenth year was marked by family tragedy and a major journey.

His dear sister, Sarah, died in childbirth after delivering a stillborn son. Abraham was distraught and blamed his brother-in-law, Aaron Grigsby, for failing to send for a doctor earlier. Later that year, Abraham piloted a boat down the Mississippi River, traveling 1,222 miles and experiencing New Orleans for the first time. This trip was potentially his first encounter with slave auctions and slavery on a large scale. Abraham later spoke of his eye-opening experience in New Orleans—a truly international city but one marred by the scourge of slavery—as a turning point.

When Abraham Lincoln was twenty-three, he volunteered in the Illinois Militia during the Black Hawk War. He was elected captain of his company, later declaring that it gave him more pleasure than any success he had after that. Lincoln never saw combat but, in the aftermath of two battles, saw scalped corpses and helped bury dead soldiers. His limited service nonetheless had a lasting impact on his life. It provided him with

Lincoln was modest about his Black Hawk War service, joking years later that his bloodiest battles were with mosquitoes.

lifelong connections and his first experience as an elected leader.

Following his service, Lincoln focused his attention on politics. He announced his candidacy for the Illinois General Assembly in the *Sangamo Journal* in 1832. Lincoln, an admirer of Henry Clay, ran as a Whig, a party focused on modernization, manufacturing, and internal development projects. Lincoln lost the election. Undeterred, he ran again two years later and won, serving his first term in the Illinois House of Representatives in 1834.

While serving as state representative, he was encouraged to study law by John Todd Stuart, who had served with him in the Black Hawk War and in the legislature. Lincoln never attended law school. The only requirement to practice law was to obtain a certificate from an Illinois county court certifying one's good moral character. Lincoln obtained his license in 1836, the same year he won a second term as a state representative.

In 1837, Lincoln moved to Springfield,

John Todd Stuart was Lincoln's first law partner and his future wife's cousin.

Illinois, with dreams of setting up a successful law practice but little money. There he began his lifelong friendship with Joshua Speed. He intended to purchase furniture in Speed's store, but when it became clear Lincoln couldn't afford any, Speed invited him to stay as his roommate. Lincoln took his few saddlebags upstairs, happily declaring that he had finished his move. Around this time, Lincoln's ill-fated engagement to a woman named Mary Owens came to an end. That same year, Lincoln made his first public antislavery address. In it, he outlined his fervent conviction that slavery was morally wrong but conceded that the Constitution protected the rights of slave owners.

During his third term as a state representative, he met the woman who would change his life. Mary Todd had moved from Lexington, Kentucky, in 1839 to live with her older sister Elizabeth and her husband, Ninian Edwards. Mary came from a wealthy family, had a superior education, was fluent in French, and had

Some claim Lincoln's first love was a woman named Ann Rutledge and that her death caused a serious bout of depression.

been neighbors with Lincoln's political idol, Henry Clay. She immediately attracted a bevy of suitors, including Lincoln.

Abraham and Mary seemed a mismatch. Compared to Mary's other suitors, Abraham was uncultured, unsophisticated, and undereducated. Yet Mary saw in him the promise of greatness and hitched her wagon to his star. Within a year of meeting they were engaged, only to have their engagement end on January 1, 1841, due to the pressure of the disapproval of Mary's family. Abraham and Mary avoided one another for over a year but then resumed their courtship.

Shortly after reuniting, Abraham became embroiled in a situation of Mary's unintentional making. Abraham wrote a satirical letter under a pseudonym in the *Sangamo Journal* poking fun at state auditor James Shields. Shields demanded a retraction. Coincidentally and without Lincoln's foreknowledge, another satirical piece was published under a pseudonym, by Mary. Infuriated, Shields challenged

As president, Lincoln enjoyed political satirists such as Charles Farrar Browne and David Ross Locke.

Lincoln to a duel. Lincoln chose broad-swords as their dueling weapons. When they arrived for the duel, Lincoln demonstrated his strength and reach by swinging his sword above the five-foot-nine-inch Shields' head and slashing a tree branch. The men called a truce.

Abraham and Mary wed on November 4, 1842, in the Edwards' house where they had first met. The Lincolns' first home together was a single room in a boarding-house called the Globe Tavern. There, Mary gave birth to their first child, Robert Todd Lincoln, on August 1, 1843. It's hard to imagine the anxiety that may have filled Abraham, given his own sister's fate in childbirth. The Lincolns next rented a small home before purchasing their first and only house together on the corner of Eighth and Jackson Streets.

As Abraham built his law practice and political standing, the Lincoln family also grew. Mary gave birth to their son Edward "Eddie" Baker Lincoln on March 10, 1846. As a lawyer with the Eighth Circuit,

Eddie was named for his parents' friend, Edward Dickinson Baker, later the only U.S. senator to be killed while serving in the Civil War.

Abraham left for several weeks at a time to ride an estimated 500-mile loop to try cases, leaving Mary alone to care for their young boys.

Lincoln's hard work paid off, and in 1846 he was elected to the United States House of Representatives. Mary, who had been instrumental in her husband's success, and their sons came with him to Washington. The Lincolns' decision was unusual—most congressmen came to Washington alone. The family lived at Mrs. Sprigg's boardinghouse, also known as "Abolition House." A fellow boarder was Joshua Giddings, a radical antislavery congressman and a future founder of the Republican Party. Lincoln relished his work but found his wife and sons distracting, yet, when Mary took the boys to live with the Todds in Kentucky, he wrote of how much he missed them and their distractions.

Though Lincoln had little power as a freshman congressman, he was a vocal opponent of what Whigs saw as the unnecessary and unconstitutional Mexican-American War. This position made him unpopular in his home district, so he kept his promise not to seek a second term. Lincoln also championed a resolution by Joshua Giddings that called for a repeal of slave trading in the District of Columbia. The federal capital was one place Congress had the power—if not the will—to end slavery.

Lincoln was horrified by how prevalent slavery was in Washington. From the Capitol, he could see enslaved people, shackled together, being marched to slave auctions.

The Lincolns reunited with family and friends in Springfield. The years that followed contained dramatic swings between highs and lows for Abraham and Mary. Their son Eddie died a few weeks before his fourth birthday, on February 1, 1850. Their grief turned to joy when they welcomed their third son, William "Willie" Wallace Lincoln on December 21, 1850. Their fourth son, Thomas "Tad" Lincoln, named for Abraham's father, was born April 4, 1853.

Abraham was notoriously permissive with his children. His law partner, William Herndon, later recollected that the boys would tear apart their law offices, with Lincoln not seeming to care one bit. Abraham's success allowed him to spend more time with his two youngest sons. Making up for lost time with his son Robert would prove difficult: by age sixteen, Robert was sent east to boarding school. Abraham was eager to provide his sons with the education he never had.

After years of career growth, Lincoln suffered a series of setbacks. In 1855, he came within five votes of becoming a U.S. senator, a seat previously held by Shields, his would-be dueling opponent, but lost. Then the Whig Party collapsed. Lincoln and other antislavery Whigs joined the newly formed Republican Party. As a Republican candidate for U.S. Senate in 1858, he was defeated by Democrat Stephen A. Douglas. The Lincoln-Douglas debates are held up as a seminal series even today. They showcased Lincoln's legendary sense of humor and storytelling while demonstrating his political savvy.

For the majority of the young nation's

existence prior to 1860, the balance of power was held by Southerners. Following James Buchanan's unpopular presidency and an economic shift toward industry in the North, the Democratic Party divided along Northern and Southern lines. In 1860, Lincoln's old rival, Stephen Douglas, became the presidential candidate for the Northern Democrats. Going into the 1860 Republican National Convention, Lincoln was a long-shot candidate, yet he snatched the nomination from political veteran and New York senator William H. Seward. A fourth party also emerged. Secession and slavery were key issues during the campaign, but many believed the talk of secession was overblown campaign rhetoric.

In response to being called "two-faced," Lincoln famously retorted, "If I had two faces, would I be wearing this one?"

Lincoln won the national election with a majority of electoral votes but failed to win a single state in the South. What should have been a triumphant moment for him and his family became a national crisis. Southern slaveholding states began issuing articles of secession and forming the Confederate States of America. Their principal fear was that an antislavery Republican administration would threaten their state-granted right to own slaves. Lincoln knew he faced a deeply divided country, and he attempted to reflect that in his cabinet appointments. His efforts did little to ebb the tide of secession. By the time the Lincolns arrived in Washington for the March inauguration, seven states had seceded. Pointedly, the Confederacy's constitution explicitly outlined protections for owning African American slaves.

Although he had won the presidency, Lincoln lacked a popular majority. As such, he did not view his election as a mandate to immediately abolish slavery but, rather, to uphold the Constitution of the United States of America. The president's first inaugural address struck a conciliatory tone:

> *"We are not enemies, but friends.*
> *We must not be enemies. Though*

Even before his inauguration, Lincoln received threats to his life and safety.

*passion may have strained it must
not break our bonds of affection.
The mystic chords of memory,
stretching from every battlefield
and patriot grave to every living
heart and hearthstone all over
this broad land, will yet swell the
chorus of the Union, when again
touched, as surely they will be, by
the better angels of our nature."*

The states in rebellion were unmoved by President Lincoln's words. Lincoln remained resolute in his view that secession was unconstitutional. If states could secede whenever they did not like the outcome of a federal election, the United States would eventually cease to exist. Lincoln understood that secession threatened the nation's great experiment in democracy and the individual liberties it bestowed and protected.

President Lincoln faced an unprecedented crisis. Secessionist rhetoric was not new, but articles of secession and mil-

In 1860, the United States was the only existing constitutional democracy in the world. Many European monarchs both expected and hoped it would fail.

itary aggression, such as the Confederate attack on Fort Sumter five weeks after Lincoln took the oath of office in 1861, were. Lincoln himself had scant military experience and was now commander in chief of a nation at war with itself. Meanwhile, some of the country's top military leaders had signed on with the Confederacy. Like countless others, the Lincolns had family on both sides of the conflict. Abraham even offered a position to Benjamin Hardin Helm, husband of Mary's favorite little sister, Emilie. Not only did Helm decline the offer, he became a Confederate officer.

Throughout the war, Lincoln had to maintain a difficult balancing act. He faced pressure in his own party to acknowledge the war was about slavery and to abolish slavery. Yet he faced the real threat of losing the slaveholding border states to the Confederacy, which would have immediately surrounded the federal capital with enemy territory. Lincoln stated that, as much as he personally ab-

Britain and France had outlawed slavery, which would have made it impossible for them to openly support the Confederacy in a war over slavery.

horred slavery, his principal responsibility was to maintain the Union—making the Civil War a war of abolition had momentous strategic implications.

In the midst of national suffering, the Lincolns were struck with another personal tragedy. Willie Lincoln fell ill and died on February 20, 1862. The cause of death is generally considered to be typhoid fever from contaminated drinking water at the Executive Mansion, as the White House was then known. Tad also fell ill but recovered. The parents were in despair at the loss of another son. By many accounts, Willie had been the most like his father in temperament, personality, and intellect. Abraham Lincoln is said to have mournfully proclaimed, "My poor boy. He was too good for this earth." While the president worked to contain his grief, Mary became consumed by hers. She attempted to keep the boys' former playmates away, finding their presence a painful reminder of the loss of her own son. As she withdrew, Tad spent more time with

Abraham Lincoln visited his son's grave often throughout the war.

his father, sometimes climbing onto him in the middle of meetings. Robert, their eldest, returned to school at Harvard.

In June of 1862, the Lincoln family moved to a cottage located three miles north of the Executive Mansion on the grounds of the Soldiers' Home. Perched on a hilltop, the site had the advantage of cool breezes to temper the summer heat. While the new home provided privacy and perspective they could not get at the Executive Mansion, it immersed the family in the consequences of war. Their neighbors included 100–200 disabled veterans. Thousands of graves multiplied at the first national cemetery for soldiers, a couple hundred yards from their front door. On the president's daily commute to and from the Executive Mansion, he encountered caravans of wounded soldiers coming back from the front line and refugee camps housing formerly enslaved men, women, and children.

That summer, Lincoln began writing the Emancipation Proclamation. His Cabinet

The Soldiers' Home was founded in 1851 by three men, including future president of the Confederacy Jefferson Davis.

urged him to release it only after a Union victory, lest it appear an act of desperation. After the Battle of Antietam, Lincoln framed the outcome to his Cabinet as predetermination, stating he had made a vow before God to issue it if General Robert E. Lee was driven back from Maryland. He issued the preliminary proclamation on September 22, 1862. The Emancipation Proclamation was enacted on January 1, 1863. Upon signing it, he said:

> *"If my name ever goes into history it will be for this act, and my whole soul is in it."*

Lincoln's Emancipation Proclamation was attacked by both sides. Some lamented that it only pertained to states in rebellion, leaving slavery in the border states untouched. Others saw it as an empty threat. Still more used it as a rallying cry against Lincoln, seeing it as vindication for secession while playing on white fears of slave rebellions.

The Emancipation Proclamation provided for the arming of black soldiers, and the United States Colored Troops were formed several months later.

Lincoln continued to express frustration with his generals. Early in the war, General George B. McClellan earned Lincoln's ire with his failure to act, insisting his horses and men were tired and he needed reinforcements. Lincoln retorted by asking what he had done since Antietam that could fatigue anything. In the summer of 1863, the Confederacy invaded the North, culminating in the Battle of Gettysburg and a staggering number of casualties. Lee was forced into retreat, but to Lincoln's frustration, his generals failed to pursue Lee, thereby prolonging the war. Casualties were not abstract for Lincoln—he saw burials regularly at the Soldiers' Home. In his Gettysburg Address, Lincoln invoked the founding fathers' vision and asserted that Union soldiers had not died in vain.

As President Lincoln's reelection loomed on the horizon in 1864, the end of the war was nowhere in sight. He had been pleased with General Ulysses S. Grant's command. Progress had been

Lincoln's Gettysburg Address lasted mere minutes, compared to renowned orator Edward Everett's address, which came first and lasted nearly two hours.

made, only for the Union to experience more setbacks. Confederate General Jubal Early attacked Washington in July, resulting in a fresh round of tirades against Lincoln's leadership. Weary of the protracted war, many feared Lincoln would not accept peace without emancipation. In a move that reveals his pragmatism and integrity, Lincoln wrote a blind memo that he asked each Cabinet member to sign. In it, he outlined his plan to work with the president-elect to save the Union in the interim period between the election and inauguration.

Jubal Early attacked Washington about a mile north of where the Lincolns lived at the Soldiers' Home, forcing them to evacuate to the Executive Mansion.

To broaden their appeal with voters, Republicans created a bipartisan ticket in 1864, replacing existing Republican Vice President and New England abolitionist Hannibal Hamlin with Andrew Johnson, a Southern Democrat who supported the war. Aided by a string of Union victories, the strategy worked and Lincoln won re-election in 1864.

Lincoln delivered his second inaugural address on March 4, 1865. Victory seemed within the Union's grasp. The Thirteenth Amendment banning slavery, which Lincoln fervently supported, had passed in both chambers of Congress. In his speech, Lincoln expressed hope the war would end soon, yet he suggested that it may be God's will that every drop of blood "drawn with the lash shall be paid by another drawn with the sword." He acknowledged the whole country had been complicit in slavery, but that one side strove for its demise while the other strove to ensure it would continue. Nonetheless, he ended by stressing that everyone must move forward together as one nation.

Lincoln was a religious skeptic in his youth but had a command of the Bible and saw its value in explaining the war.

"With malice toward none, with charity for all, with firmness in the right as God gives us to see the right, let us strive on to finish the work we are in, to bind up the nation's wounds, to care for him who shall have borne the battle and for his widow and his orphan, to do all which may achieve and

*cherish a just and lasting peace
among ourselves and with all
nations."*

On April 9, 1865, Lee surrendered to Grant at Appomattox. The Union was victorious. Crowds rallied at the Executive Mansion two days later, imploring Lincoln to give a speech. Reporters were present, and Tad Lincoln held the pages of the speech as his father discarded each one while reading from a second-floor window. It was the first time Lincoln publicly expressed his support for black suffrage. Actor John Wilkes Booth stood in the crowd, fuming, and vowed Lincoln's speech would be his last.

Abraham and Mary Lincoln went on a carriage ride around the city on April 13. They spoke of putting aside their suffering, of enjoying life. The next evening, on Good Friday, they attended a comedy at Ford's Theatre. Clara Harris and Major Henry Rathbone joined them in the presidential box. Then, during a moment when

Lincoln's guard was away, Booth slipped into the box and shot Abraham Lincoln in the head.

One of Booth's co-conspirators, part of a coordinated effort to eliminate Union leadership, managed to stab Secretary of State William Seward at his home, but Seward survived relatively unharmed.

Pandemonium ensued as Booth made his escape, only to be caught and killed twelve days later. Meanwhile, witnesses carried the president to a boardinghouse across the street. Mary Lincoln was in hysterics, having witnessed firsthand her husband's gruesome murder. Robert Lincoln was summoned and stayed with his father at Petersen House throughout the night. The following morning, April 15, President Lincoln was declared dead. He was fifty-six years old.

The nation, jubilant a day before, was plunged into shock and grief. Three days later, President Lincoln lay in state in the East Room of the White House. The funeral train departed Washington on April 21, 1865, carrying the remains of both Abraham and Willie Lincoln. The train made eleven official stops along the way, ending in Springfield, Illinois. Mary, Robert, and Tad stayed behind in Washington.

During his presidency, Abraham Lincoln was criticized as much as he was praised. Following his assassination, he was heralded as a martyr. For decades, monuments and memorials were erected in his honor in the United States and around the world. Not only did he manage to "save the Union" but he put legal slavery on the road to extinction, expanded the nation's railroads and infrastructure, encouraged immigration, created the Department of Agriculture, and supported legislation that expanded access to livelihood and education.

Lincoln's legacy has not been without controversy. Many citizens in former Confederate states clung to the "lost cause" rhetoric that recast their struggle as noble and denounced Lincoln as a tyrant. In the mid-twentieth century, some argued that Lincoln was a racist, reluctant emancipator. Nevertheless, he is routinely ranked among the most popular U.S. presidents. He is frequently depicted in pop culture, art, and literature. Interest in him

Abraham Lincoln's last direct descendant, Robert Todd Lincoln Beckwith, died in 1985.

Abraham
Lincoln is
among
the most-
written-
about
subjects
in human
history. skyrocketed with the bicentennial of his birth in 2009. Lincoln's story continues to captivate people around the world, and it inspires hope that unity and freedom will always prevail.

raham Lincoln Abraham Linco
incoln Abraham Lincoln Abra
braham Lincoln Abraham Linco
incoln Abraham Lincoln Abra
braham Lincoln Abraham Linco
incoln Abraham Lincoln Abra
braham Lincoln Abraham Linco
incoln Abraham Lincoln Abra
braham Lincoln Abraham Linco
incoln Abraham Lincoln Abra
braham Lincoln Abraham Linco
incoln Abraham Lincoln Abra
braham Lincoln Abraham Linco
incoln Abraham Lincoln Abra
braham Lincoln Abraham Linco
incoln Abraham Lincoln Abra
braham Lincoln Abraham Linco
incoln Abraham Lincoln Abra
braham Lincoln Abraham Linc

raham Lincoln Abraham Linco
ncoln Abraham Lincoln Abra
raham Lincoln Abraham Linco
ncoln Abraham Lincoln Abra
raham Lincoln Abraham Linco
ncoln Abraham Lincoln Abra
raham Lincoln Abraham Linco
ncoln Abraham Lincoln Abra
raham Lincoln Abraham Linco
ncoln Abraham Lincoln Abra
raham Lincoln Abraham Linco
ncoln Abraham Lincoln Abra
raham Lincoln Abraham Linco
ncoln Abraham Lincoln Abra
raham Lincoln Abraham Linco
ncoln Abraham Lincoln Abra
raham Lincoln Abraham Linco
ncoln Abraham Lincoln Abra
raham Lincoln Abraham Linco